A Long Way Home

by
Anna Imgrund

GLOBE FEARON
Pearson Learning Group

Project Editor: Brian Hawkes

Editorial Assistants: Jennifer Keezer, Jenna Thorsland

Editorial Development: ELHI Publishers, LLC

Art Supervision: Sharon Ferguson

Production Editor: Regina McAloney

Electronic Page Production: Debbie Childers

Manufacturing Supervisor: Mark Cirillo

Cover Design: Sharon Ferguson

Illustrator: Charles Shaw

ISBN 0-130-23295-5
Printed in the United States of America

6 7 8 9 10 11   07 06 05 04 03 02

Globe
Fearon

Pearson Learning Group

1-800-321-3106
www.pearsonlearning.com

Contents

1. Somewhere in South America 5

2. Looking Back 8

3. Meanwhile, in California 13

4. Hope Comes to Camp 18

5. To the U.S. 23

6. Back to Life 27

7. A Change of Mind 32

8. The Big Question 37

9. If It Feels Good, Do It 41

10. A Star in the Making 45

11. On the News 49

12. Sisters 52

13. Miss Politics 54

14. Back to Work 58

1. Somewhere in South America

The dark, thin girl stands off to the side, away from all the others, and looks out over the sea of tents. This camp is a big one, much bigger than the last, but she sees on every face the same lost look. It is a look without hope. It is a look that has seen too many camps, too many people, and too much hurt.

How did it come to this? the girl asks herself. *What happened to my life, my family, my home?* She sits down on the ground, knowing that there will be no dinner tonight. There is never enough food. There are never enough blankets. And always, always, there are too many people.

"What are you doing over here, Carmen?" asks Inez, walking up to her. "You know it's not good to go so far from the fires as night falls."

"I wanted to be by myself," says Carmen, "to think."

"Sometimes, these days, it's good not to think too much," says Inez. "And it is never, **never** good to be by yourself. Not here."

"I know," says Carmen. "But what can anyone do to me now?"

"You must have hope, Carmen," says Inez. "Do not give up!"

"Why not?" asks Carmen. "I have nothing else to lose."

"You have **you**," says Inez, sitting down next to her. "You have what's here, what's inside," she says, pointing to Carmen. "Do not let them take that from you. Anything else, but not that."

Carmen puts her head down on her arms and cries. "It's too late, Inez," she gets out. "It's just too late for me."

Inez, too, begins to cry. "It's all right, Carmen," she says, putting her arm around her friend. "We can cry. But we **cannot** give up."

With that, Inez gets up from the ground and turns to walk back to her tent. "Try not to be out long, Carmen," she calls back. "It's not safe in the dark."

Carmen looks up at the stars in the night sky. *Nothing is different out there,* she thinks. *How can so much have changed for me?* She puts her head back down and gives in to her feelings. Without wanting to, without trying, her mind goes back to the point where things went so very wrong. It goes back to the night in the fields.

2. Looking Back

Dad had just come home from working in the mine. Mom was cooking dinner, and Carmen had been helping the boys with their schoolwork. The family was happy, Carmen remembers. The mining was going well. Gold had hit its highest point in history! Everyone said it was going to make for a new South America, a new way of life! And César Cruz, Carmen's dad, had believed it.

Talk that not everyone was happy with the news did not scare CésarCruz. "Those men will see!" he would laugh. "When the money comes in, and they can pay the bills, and there are no more sharecroppers — **then** they will come around! It will be fine, little Carmen," Dad would say. "It will all work out."

"Oh, Dad!" Carmen had said. "I am not a little girl! I am 16 years old now!"

"You are **my** 16-year-old little girl, then!" Dad had laughed. "And someday you will be 26, and 36, and 46 years old. Even then," Dad had said, "you will be my little girl."

Carmen smiles at the memory. It seems like it was only a day or two ago, but it was really 13 or 14 weeks back—a lifetime. Carmen doesn't know if it is the night or the cold memory that moves her, but she gets out the only thing she owns in the camp—a small cloth blanket—and pulls it around her.

Again, her mind goes back to that night. *It will be fine, little Carmen*, Dad had said. But he had been wrong. For the first time in her life, Carmen saw that CésarCruz could be wrong. Things would **not** be OK. In fact, after that night, things would never be OK again.

Is there anything that could have been different? Mom had still been cooking dinner when the men came. Dad had been talking to the boys, so Carmen put their schoolwork aside. But as she stood up, she and Mom had heard a sound.

"What was that?" Carmen's mom had asked.

"I didn't hear anything," said Dad, who was telling the boys a joke.

Again, there were small sounds. Then bigger sounds. Then people calling out!

Carmen remembers Dad laughing. "I think the boys from the mine have started to count their money a little too fast! It sounds like they have been drinking their pay!"

But no one was laughing at what happened next. A man had hit the door three times, calling out, "Open up! Open up right now!" Before the family could even move, two other men hit the door so hard that it crashed down.

"What is this?!" cried CésarCruz, who stood up fast. He pushed the boys behind him and put out his hand for Carmen.

"Is your name Cruz? **César**Cruz?" the men asked.

"Who wants to know?" Carmen's dad came back. But they had not liked that answer, not at all, and had hit Carmen's dad over the head so hard that it had thrown him on the ground. "Take him!" one of the men had ordered. "Take them **all** out with the others!"

Carmen's mom then screamed as man after man had come into their home, where they had always been safe, and pulled them all outside.

"Run! Run for your lives!"

There, in the night, Carmen had seen people being pushed to the field where she and her friends played stickball every day. And over in that field Carmen heard screams that said life as they had known it was over. *What was going to happen to them all?* she wanted to know. Then, somehow, she knew.

"Run!" she called out in a bold move. "Run for your lives!" With that, Carmen had pulled free of a man who had his hands on her arm, and raced for the woods. "Run!" she had screamed again and again as she raced, scared to look back and even more scared of what was ahead. For miles and miles, Carmen screamed and ran.

Thinking back on it, Carmen can't believe she got away that night. But remembering is hard, and she shakes her head as if that could make the memory go away. She sits on the hard earth in camp, her eyes moving over the tents, the people, and the ruin of the place she now calls home. At last, she looks back up to the sky. *I will go on*, she says to herself. *Like the stars, I will go on.*

3. Meanwhile, in California

"Kay!" calls her mom. "Robin is here!"

"Coming!" says Kay, putting on her backpack as she walks into the kitchen.

"What are you two girls up to today?" Mom asks.

"Not much, Mrs. White," says Robin.

"Not much?" says Kay, looking at her friend. "What are you talking about? We have an EarthSave meeting in study hall at 2:00, and we are going to work at the Friends 4 Life homeless shelter after school!"

Robin just laughs. "Sorry, Mrs. White," she says. "What I **should** have said is that we are saving the planet today."

"No, no, Robin," says Kay with a smile, turning to look at her friend. "First California, then the U.S., and **then** the planet."

They all laugh. Around school, Kay White is known as Miss Politics, Head of All Good Causes!

"Is there any cause you **have not** taken up, Kay?" asks Mom.

"Well," says Kay, "I was not real big in the Sharks Are Our Friends group, but that was only because you would not let me."

"I never said that," Mom comes back. "All I said was that you could not keep a shark in the house!"

"He was sick," says Kay.

"He was a shark," says Mom.

"OK, he was a sick shark," laughs Kay. "Anyway, it didn't give me a lot of points with that group."

"What about the Insects Have Feelings Too push?" asks Robin. "Remember that one, Mrs. White?"

"You know I do," says Mom. "I was thinking Kay was going to call the police when her dad went to kill the ants out front."

"I was!" says Kay. "The ants had a right to live where they wanted to."

"But, Kay," says Mom, "too many of them wanted to live right outside your bedroom window!"

"I know," Kay says. "That **was** a problem."

"And it got to be an even bigger problem," laughs Robin, "when the ants got into your room!"

"I did learn not to eat crackers right before you go to sleep," says Kay. "Not if ants are around, anyway."

"In summary," says Mom, "I think it's safe to say that you have taken **some** causes just a little too far."

"But the ones we are going to work on today are really good ones, Mom," says Kay. "EarthSave is all about cleaning up the freeway and keeping the air clean."

"What about Friends 4 Life?" asks Mom.

"That's a shelter for families," says Kay. "We want to raise money to build a new playground."

"Well, girls," says Mrs. White, "that's a big job, but it looks like they have the right kids working on it."

"We are not the only ones," Robin tells her. "Guy, Mu Lan, and Mack are coming to the meetings too."

"And I think maybe Mr. Goldman, our principal, is going to help with the shelter," says Kay. "That's why we need to meet after school."

"Oh, man!" screams Robin. "Look at the time! We are going to be late for history class, Kay!"

"But—," Mom starts to say.

"You don't need to come for me after the meeting, Mom," Kay calls as she gets her last book from the living room. "I'll walk home."

"That's fine," says Mom, "but—."

"Oh, and don't save dinner for me," Kay says as she runs out the door, pushing a book into her backpack. "I'll just get something when I come home."

"But, Kay, do you think—?"

"See you, Mrs. White!" calls Robin.

"See you, Mom!" calls Kay.

Mrs. White, smiling, gives up at last and stands in the doorway. She waves at the two girls, keeping her eyes on them as they make their way to school. When they turn the corner, she shakes her head and laughs. "I'm so happy they can get Kay to clean up the freeways," she says to herself. "I can't even get her to clean up her room!"

From the corner of her eye, she sees Mr. Rivet walking up to the house with a pack of letters and ads for her. "Here you go, Mrs. White," says the big, smiling man. "Lots of news for you today, I see," he says.

"Good news, I hope," laughs Mrs. White, taking the letters from Mr. Rivet and waving to him before she goes back to the kitchen. She smiles again about the two girls and their many causes as she starts to look through the letters, bills, and ads in her hand. But it doesn't take long for the name on one letter to register with Mrs. White.

"Oh, good!" she says. "Something from the Cruz family!" Happily, she opens that one first, thinking about how long it's been since the Whites have heard from their South American friends. All too soon, her happy smile leaves her face as she tries to take in the meaning of the words:

Mr. and Mrs. White,

Can you help me? Much killing here! Family gone! I am in a camp. Not safe. No other place to turn! Help!

Carmen Cruz

4. Hope Comes to Camp

The weeks go by in South America, and little changes. Carmen sits outside a tent, waiting for the truck that everyone hopes will bring food and clean water. A new girl came into camp today, and all of the women are asking her questions. *Have you been to this camp or that one? Did you see my husband? Have you heard the name of so-and-so?* Carmen asked many questions at one time, too, but she has given up. Her family is gone.

Inez comes over and sits down by her. "What did you do to your hand?" she asks.

"I just have some cuts," says Carmen as she takes the corner of her blanket and puts it in water, then up against her hurt hand to clean it.

Inez looks at Carmen. "It was those boys, right?" she asks. "You were trying to keep away from those boys at the far end of camp."

"It's OK," says Carmen. "It worked." Wanting to talk about something else, Carmen asks, "Did the new girl have any news to tell you?"

"No," says Inez, shaking her head. She looks so sad. Her boyfriend Luis had been taken, as well as her family. Inez herself, who had been working that day, had gotten away. Now she is scared that none of those who were taken are alive. "The new girl knew nothing," Inez goes on. "There are just too many people in too many camps."

"What about the mining?" asks Carmen. "Has it started again? Maybe they are keeping Dad and the other miners safe so that they can work again!"

Inez looks at Carmen, then shakes her head. "This is not about gold, my friend," says Inez, taking Carmen's hand. "This is about who will run things for us all. Gold just got things started. Remember, Carmen, wherever there is money for some but not for all, there will be problems and fights."

"So you don't think they are keeping my dad and the others safe somewhere?" Carmen wants to know.

Inez gives her a long look. At last she says, "No. No, I don't."

Carmen looks down, wanting to cry but knowing that Inez is right.

"What can we do?" asks Carmen.

"What else?" says Inez. "We have to start over." They sit together, not talking, for some time. Inez finds a stick and starts writing on the ground as she thinks. At last, she looks up. "You know, Carmen," she says. "They say there is a good life in the U.S. They say that even the poor can go to work, and if they work hard enough, they can be somebody."

"Did I tell you my dad has some friends in the U.S.?" Carmen asks Inez. "Good friends."

"Then you should ask them for help," says Inez. "They may be your best hope."

"All the hope I have in the world could be put into a ring box," Carmen says with a sad smile, "and there **still** could be room besides." She looks around the camp at wall-to-wall people with no water, no food, and, like herself, little hope. "My mom used to tell me that I was going to be someone someday," Carmen says. "She always said that good things would happen to me." She laughs in a sad, sad way. "How wrong Mom was!"

"She was not wrong," Inez tells her. "You **are** somebody, Carmen, even now. Even here, in a South American camp, **you are somebody**. Do not ever forget this!"

Carmen smiles at the woman who has come to mean so much in this bad place and time in her life. "What I will not forget, Inez, is how kind you are," she says. "Forgive me for being so down about everything."

"Have you tried to get word to your friends in the U.S.?" asks Inez.

"I sent a letter," says Carmen, "but the only way I could get it out of camp was to give it to a thief who was thrown out weeks ago. It was the only thing I could think to do. Who knows if he really sent it for me?"

Inez just laughs. "If they throw everyone out who steals," she says, "then there will be no camp at all!" But she sees that Carmen is scared. "Don't be scared, Carmen," she says. "He sent it."

"How do you know?" asks Carmen.

"Because I feel it," says Inez with a smile. "Now, come on." She gets up, putting her hand out to Carmen. "If the food trucks **do** get here, we will need to have firewood."

Carmen uses a big walking stick to help her stand. She has been too long without food and is no longer strong. She and Inez hold each other up as they go look for firewood, keeping their eyes open for the gangs of people who could harm them. From the far end of camp, they hear many voices but think nothing of it.

As they walk, however, the voices start to build. "She's over there," Inez hears someone say. Then, "small girl with dark hair?" asks another. "That way!" cries still another.

Before they know it, the voices are coming toward Carmen and Inez. *Should they run?* Carmen turns to see many people running toward her. *I cannot run again*, she thinks. *I'm not strong enough.*

Out of the sea of faces, she sees one that tells her everything will be all right. "Mrs. White!" Carmen screams. "It's me! Carmen!"

Mrs. White's eyes grow big as it registers that this girl, who looks as if she has not had food in weeks, is the same Carmen she knows. Then, just as fast, she has to shake that memory off. "I'm here, Carmen!" Mrs. White calls out, not wanting to cry. She runs to the girl's side, and Carmen falls into her arms, knowing now that somehow, some way, the world will be right again.

5. To the U.S.

Mrs. White gets off the freeway as she drives home, and pulls her car over to the side. She turns to the girl in the car with her, whose dark eyes seem to be closed against this new place.

"Are you scared?" she asks, taking the girl's hand.

"A little," Carmen says, looking at Mrs. White and trying to smile.

"You have been through a lot, Carmen," Mrs. White tells her. "It will take time for you to get used to the U.S., even though you **do** talk very well. That's a start! It will take more than that, I guess, to get over all that has happened. You know we will do what we can to help."

"I know, Mrs. White," says Carmen, starting to cry. "I don't mean to act this way."

"There is no **right** way to act after what you have had to face," Mrs. White says. "Just be yourself, Carmen. You're free now." She looks over at the girl, still so small and scared, and hopes that a new life in the U.S. will bring a smile to her face again someday. "OK, Carmen," Mrs. White says, turning the car back on. "Let's go home."

Before they get to the family's neighborhood, they drive by Kay's school and by Mr. White's office. Having lived around farms and mining all her life, Carmen can see that this is all very different.

"We are almost home," says Mrs. White as she turns onto Goodnight Drive. "Our house is the one at the end." She points to a pretty yellow house with a white door and white windows. There are two girls sitting out front, who look up and wave. *It looks like a painting,* thinks Carmen. *Can this be real? Am I going to open my eyes and find that I'm still in camp?*

The two girls out front get up as Mrs. White pulls into the driveway.

"Welcome home," one of them says. Carmen remembers Kay from pictures the Whites have sent to the Cruz family over the years.

"Kay, Robin, this is Carmen," says Mrs. White.

Kay and Robin wave to the girl getting out of the car, a girl with the darkest hair and eyes they have ever seen. She looks so small, as if she needs to eat — fast! "Hi, Carmen," they say happily. Then, like most American girls, they start asking questions and talking so fast that Carmen cannot understand everything. She looks from one girl to the other, not knowing who to answer first or what to say.

"Not so fast, kids," says Mom, seeing the problem. "Slow down and give Carmen some time to get used to us!"

"OK, Mom, we'll try," says Kay. Then she turns to Carmen. "Do you want to go somewhere with Robin and me?" she asks.

Carmen looks at Robin and tries to smile, but shakes her head. "No," she says. "But you go on. It is OK."

Kay tries again. "How about this, Carmen? We'll go up to the Cook's Wagon and get a hot dog! They are really good."

"I don't think so," Carmen says again. "I will wait here."

"Well, then," says Kay, trying to think of something Carmen would like, "would you like to go up to the school? There are lots of people there."

"No!" screams Carmen. "No people! Not now! Not ever!" And with that, she runs from them all to the door of the pretty yellow house.

6. Back to Life

"Just try to understand," Mom says to Kay after dinner one night. Carmen has been with them for weeks now, but she says little and keeps to herself. "Remember," Mrs. White says, "Carmen has been through a lot."

"Like what?" asks Kay.

"I don't want to say," says Mom. "I don't even know everything. Just take my word for it. She has had a bad time."

"And her family?" asks Kay. "Any word?"

Mrs. White stops putting the dinner things away. She looks at Kay and shakes her head. "For now, **we** are her family," Mom says. "And we do what all families do. We help each other."

"What do you mean, **help** her?" asks Kay. "She doesn't seem to want anything to do with me! Besides, you know that Friends 4 Life and EarthSave are taking a lot of my time."

"Just show Carmen around," Mom says. "Talk to her, let her meet your friends, things like that."

"If you say so, Mom," says Kay. "But it goes two ways, and I don't think she's interested."

Kay leaves her mom in the kitchen, and goes to find Carmen. It's not hard. So far, the South American girl keeps to her room.

As Kay walks by the door of Carmen's room, she sees the girl standing by the window, looking out at the night. *Better give it another try*, thinks Kay. "What's up?" she asks, walking into the room.

Carmen, who didn't see Kay in the door, screams and falls down, putting her arms over her head as if Kay were going to beat her!

"It's OK, Carmen, it's just me," says Kay. She runs over to the girl, who is shaking. "I'm sorry, Carmen," Kay says. "I didn't mean to scare you."

Carmen gets back up and turns to Kay, "D-D-Did you need me?" she asks.

"It's OK, Carmen, it's just me," says Kay.

"Yes, I do!" Kay tells her. "Robin will be here in a little while, and we are going out to raise money for a shelter. Come with us!"

"No, I don't think so," says Carmen. She points to a book on the nightstand. "I was going to read."

"Oh, come on," says Kay. "You can read anytime."

But Carmen is not going anywhere. "No," she says.

"Look," Kay tells her, "you can't close yourself up in here like an outlaw or something!"

"I am not an outlaw!" says Carmen.

"Then don't act like one!" says Kay. "Enough hiding! I know it's been hard for you, Carmen, but life goes on! There are people out there who need your help, so get your jeans on and let's go help!"

Kay walks out of Carmen's room and down the hall to her own room, not looking back. *Maybe I pushed too hard*, she thinks. But Carmen cannot stay in that room forever, and Kay is a little sick of it anyway. Kay puts on some jeans and gets her backpack. She is just headed back to the kitchen when she hears the front door.

"I'll get it," Kay calls out, knowing it is Robin.

"Sorry I'm late," says Robin. "Mu Lan and Mack went on ahead. They said they would meet us there."

"Is Mr. Goldman going to be there too?" asks Kay.

"I hope so," Robin tells her. "We need him badly."

"I was hoping," says Kay, "that I could get Carmen to go." She looks back down the hall. "But I guess not."

"We really can't wait," says Robin. "If we are going to raise money for the playground by cleaning cars, then we had better go."

Kay looks down the hall one more time, then gives up. *She's not coming*, Kay thinks. "OK, Robin, let's go," she says, then calls out, "Mom, we are cleaning cars at Friends 4 Life!"

The two girls race out the door and down the sidewalk. As they reach the corner, however, a small voice calls out behind them: "Kay!" calls Carmen. "Wait for me!"

7. A Change of Mind

"What made you change your mind?" asks Kay as Carmen gets to the corner.

"I don't know," says Carmen. "But you were right, Kay. I cannot hide forever." She looks around at the sunny sky and the pretty day and is happy that she is at last out of the house. It's the first time that she can feel the sun and the wind on her face in the U.S., and it feels good.

The three girls walk by the high school and head to a small building on the corner of 10th and Mississippi streets. There, out front, Carmen sees a group of high school kids working to clean a line of cars to raise money for the playground.

"Hi, Mu Lan!" Robin and Kay call out. "Hi, Mack! Hi, everyone!"

As all the workers come over, Carmen once again feels the need to run away, to hide. She turns her dark eyes on Kay, and Kay knows she feels scared.

"You don't have to work," says Kay. "Why don't you go over there and sit down by Mr. Goldman, our principal? I'll come get you when the line of cars goes down a little."

Carmen walks over to the side of the building, where a man is sitting on some wooden boxes. She starts to talk, but the words will not come out.

The man looks up. "Would you care to sit down?" he asks, pulling up another wooden box for her. "My name is Principal Goldman, but most of the kids call me Mr. G."

"I am — I am Carmen," she says.

"I don't remember seeing you up at the school, Carmen," Mr. Goldman says. "Do I know your mom and dad?"

Carmen knows that Mr. Goldman does not know about what she has been through, but the memories hurt just the same. She can't help it. Carmen starts to cry. "No," she gets out, "you do not know my mom and dad. I just moved here from South America, and I am rooming with the Whites."

Mr. Goldman feels bad. He **has** heard about this girl's sad story. "I am sorry," he says. "I didn't mean to hurt you."

They sit and talk a little more, and Carmen finds that Mr. Goldman knows a lot about South America. More than that, he knows a lot about kids. Before long, he has her laughing again.

"You know," says Mr. Goldman, "there is someone here that I think you should meet."

"Who?" asks Carmen, looking around.

"His name is Jared," says Mr. Goldman, "and I think you two would be good friends. Jared!" he calls to a guy cleaning the hood of a red VW. "Can you come here?"

"No problem, Mr. G," the kid calls back. He puts his cleaning cloth back in the water and runs over to the principal.

"Jared," says Mr. Goldman, "I would like for you to meet Carmen. She's new to the U.S. and, I hope, will be new to our school in the coming weeks."

"Hi, Carmen!" says Jared, taking in her dark eyes and pretty smile.

"Carmen here has had a bad time of it for a while, Jared. I told her that you and she might have some things to talk about."

Jared looks at the principal, who gets up to let the boy sit down. Then Mr. Goldman walks over to the line of cars to help again.

"I feel like you have been asked to keep your eye on me," says Carmen. "Really, I'm all right."

"No, it's not that," says Jared. "I have been through a bad time myself. He just—well, he just thinks that maybe I could help you through whatever it is you have had to face."

Carmen looks at this California kid, with his white teeth and laughing eyes. *What would he know about being scared?* she thinks. *What would he know about being hurt?*

"I don't think anyone can help," she says. "Not now."

"Can I try?" asks Jared. "I don't know what happened to you, but I can tell you what happened to me."

"What's that?" Carmen asks, still thinking that he could have nothing to share. "You lost a dog? You didn't pass a test? What?"

Jared, with understanding, only laughs. "My dog and my tests are fine," he says, "but my dad **did** try to burn down our house." He gives Carmen a sad smile. "And my mom and I were in it."

8. The Big Question

"Oh, Jared," Carmen says, "I am so sorry!"

"It's OK," he tells her. "I just wanted you to know that when I say I know what you're going through, those aren't just words. I have been there. I have lived it."

"Can I ask what happened?" Carmen wants to know.

"My mom and dad were fighting at the time. Dad was a big drinker." Carmen sees the hurt in his eyes as Jared thinks back. "He had hurt Mom before, but never that badly. And, every time, he would say it would never happen again. But it did, over and over and over."

"And that night?" asks Carmen.

"My dad had had a lot to drink and started taking it out on us. My mom told him to pack his bags and get out, for **good** this time. He was mad and started hitting her, but at last she got him to go. For a little while, we really were thinking everything was going to be OK."

"But he didn't go?" asks Carmen.

"He went all right," says Jared. "But he came back and started the fire. I guess he was thinking that if **he** could not have us, then **no one** could."

"How did you get out?" Carmen asks.

"My mom made her way in the dark back to my room to get me up. We had just enough time to get out a window before the fire took the house." He shakes his head, then goes on. "I was OK, but Mom had some pretty bad burns."

"What did you do?" Carmen asks.

"Mom had heard about Friends 4 Life, about how they help families with problems like ours," he says. "So Mom called Friends 4 Life. The people here saved us. They really did. That's why I'm here today and most Saturdays, helping out. And that"—Jared smiles—"is why Mr. Goldman was thinking we might have something to talk about."

Carmen looks down. She feels bad about the way she looked down on Jared, thinking that he could never have known hurt like her own. "I'm sorry, Jared," she says at last. "I forgot that I'm not the only one on the planet who has lost something."

"I know how you feel," says Jared. "But I can also tell you that it **does** get better."

"How?" Carmen asks.

"By helping someone else," says Jared, "like getting this playground for the shelter. I was not a little kid when we came here, but there are lots of them here. And you talk about scared!" he goes on. "These kids have been through so much. They come in here with their faces down, not saying a word to anyone. Some of them have never even been on a playground! But we can change that."

Carmen looks around at all the people going out of their way to help the Friends 4 Life shelter. "You know," she says, "I was starting to think that there were no good people anymore — that everyone was like the men who came to our house in South America. But" — she turns to Jared — "you and Kay have shown me that I was wrong."

"I'm happy we could do it." Jared smiles at her. "The big question now is this: What are you going to do to make things better?"

"Well," Carmen tells him as she gets up off the wooden box, "the first thing I'm going to do is find a car that needs a good cleaning."

9. If It Feels Good, Do It

As the last car pulls out of the lot, the kids all run over to Mr. Goldman and the head of Friends 4 Life, Mrs. Bills.

"How much money did we make?" asks Kay. "Is it going to be enough?"

"Hold on," says Mrs. Bills as she counts out the money. Everyone waits, hoping their hard work today was worth it.

"Well, kids," says Mrs. Bills, "with the money we raised last week on the hot dog dinner at the Cook's Wagon, we now have enough money to put in the new playground!"

The happy screams that go up from the Friends 4 Life building can be heard all the way over at the high school! Someone starts a car and turns on the radio, while everyone shakes hands and gives high 5's, making their way around the lot. "All right!" Kay calls out. "We did it, you guys!"

Carmen stands over to the side, smiling at all the people who worked together to make this happen.

"I guess I don't need this anymore," laughs Jared as he throws out the cloth he has been using to clean cars. He walks over to stand by Carmen, but she isn't saying much. *That's all right,* Jared thinks. *I can work around that.* "What's on your mind?" he asks.

"Not much," says Carmen. "It's just that you and Kay were right, Jared. It **does** feel good to help with someone else's problems. In fact, I have not been this happy in a long, long time."

"Maybe you should think about coming up here with me to help on the weekends," says Jared. "I mean, if helping one time makes you happy, then I think Mrs. Bills could make you **really, really** happy with all the work that needs to be done around here!"

"It does feel good to help with someone else's problems," says Carmen.

43

"It's an idea," Carmen says.

"Now, now, I might have something to say about that," says a voice. It's Mr. Goldman, on his way into the building with the money they have raised.

"How's that, Mr. G.?" asks Jared.

"Well, I'm hoping Carmen will get started at the high school next week, now that she feels a little more at home here. What do you think?"

"I think it's the best idea I have heard all day!" says Jared. He turns to Carmen. "Well?" he asks. "It's up to you."

"I don't know," says Carmen, looking at Mr. Goldman. "Why don't you try telling me that there is **no** homework, **long** study halls, and only the **best** food? That would be hard to turn down!"

Mr. Goldman just laughs. "How about asking for something I **can** do," he asks, "like putting you in some of Jared's classes? Would I be wrong in thinking maybe I could sell you on that?"

Carmen's face turns red as she looks at Jared, but a big smile never leaves her face. "OK, OK," she says at last. "Sold."

10. A Star in the Making

The White family cannot believe the changes in Carmen after the day she cleaned cars at Friends 4 Life. "She's like a different girl," Mrs. White tells Kay one day.

"Not different," says Kay, "just happy again."

"How do you think she's doing in school?" Mom wants to know.

"Good," says Kay, "from what I can tell. Jared has gone out of his way to help her."

"And her social life?" asks Mom. "How is that?"

Kay laughs. "Let's just say that Jared has taken it upon himself to help her with that too."

"I know she's been going with him on Saturdays to help out at the shelter."

"Yes," says Kay. "They are about to put in the new playground, too, so Carmen has been helping with that."

"She still has some hard nights, I know," says Mom in a low voice. "I walked down the hall by her room the other night and heard her cry."

"I know it's hard," says Kay. "I have heard her cry too. She misses her family a lot. I think she knows that she will never find them." Kay looks at her mom. "You know, she also had a friend in the camp named Inez. She doesn't talk about her as much anymore, but I know she thinks about Inez a lot."

"We can't change the bad things that Carmen has had to face," says Mom, her voice sad, "but I'm happy to know that she is finding a good life here in California. That would have made her dad, Cesar, very happy."

"Who's very happy?" asks Carmen as she and Jared come in through the kitchen door.

"**We** are," says Mom, giving Kay a look, "— happy that you are here, and happy that you are doing so well."

"I have had a little help," says Carmen, holding Jared's hand. "I have to hand it to these California boys," she smiles. "They know how to make a South American girl feel welcome."

"Boys?" jokes Jared. "They?"

"OK, OK," laughs Carmen. "You!"

Jared gives her a big smile, then remembers something. "Oh—guess what, Mrs. White!" says Jared. "We are going to be on TV!"

"Because you made a girl feel welcome?" Mom jokes.

"No, not that," says Carmen. "It's because of the playground! KTVN called Mrs. Bills today, and they are coming out to do a story on us!"

"But that's not all," says Jared, giving Carmen a look that says she's holding something back.

"OK, Carmen, out with it!" cry Mrs. White and Kay.

"Well, Mrs. Bills asked me to talk with the KTVN people," says Carmen. "They want to show how someone can turn a bad part of her own life into something good for others."

Mrs. White goes over to put her arms around Carmen. "I am so happy for you, Carmen," she says. "You have come a long way from the scared girl I saw in the camp."

Carmen looks down. "I **have** come a long way," says Carmen, her eyes wet. "But I still have a long way to go."

11. On the News

Donna Day, the news woman, talks to Mrs. Bills by the new playground, while someone else with KTVN puts Carmen where they want her to stand. "We need to get the best light," the woman tells her. Carmen is becoming a little sick at the idea of going on TV, but Jared is off to the side giving her a smile. *I guess I can do this*, she thinks.

At 4:30, the kids in the shelter run over to try out the playground for the first time, and the news woman comes over to talk to Carmen. Everyone smiles as they see the happy faces on the little ones.

A man says, "5, 4, 3, 2, and —." He points to Donna Day. On the air, Day says, "Here with me now is Friends 4 Life worker Carmen Cruz, who brings her own history of hard times to her work here at the shelter. Carmen, what's your story? How did you come to be a part of the playground team?"

Carmen tries to keep from shaking as she tells Day about everything that happened in South America, about the men, the camps, and her lost family. She tells how much the shelter means to her and how, in helping others, she has helped herself.

"This is Donna Day at the Friends 4 Life shelter saying, 'Good work, Carmen, and good night, California.'" The lights turn off, and the KTVN workers race off in their TV trucks, looking for the next big news story. Carmen waves to Donna Day, then walks off by herself and looks up at the pretty, sunny California sky. Jared starts to go to her, but Mrs. White gets there ahead of him.

"Are you all right, Carmen?" she asks.

The dark-eyed girl turns to the woman she now calls Mom, and takes her hand. "I will be OK," she says. "But thinking about the time that has passed, thinking about my family, is hard." Mrs. White puts her arm around Carmen as she starts to cry. "I have good days and bad," Carmen says, "but I guess the good days make the bad ones worth going through."

"Well, if you forget everything else," Mom says, "remember this: You are a part of our family now, and families are there for the good times **and** the bad. We are here for you, Carmen."

"I know," Carmen answers. "And that means a lot to me."

"Working on the playground team has been the best thing," says Mom. "Friends 4 Life needed you, Carmen, and **you** needed to be needed."

"It's good to know I can make some little kids smile," Carmen says.

Mom laughs as she looks over Carmen's head. "I may be wrong," she says, "but I would say you have put a smile on the face of more than just the little kids."

Carmen turns to see Jared standing there, with a winning smile, waiting to take her hand.

12. Sisters

The week goes by fast. All the kids in school joke about Carmen becoming a big star, now that she has had her time on KTVN.

"Keep your eye on her, Kay," Robin laughs. "Before you know it, she will be wearing dark sunglasses and the neighborhood will be trying to vote her into the White House."

"That's fine with me," Kay jokes back, "as long as she doesn't forget when it's her turn to clean up after dinner."

"I don't have to worry about that," says Carmen. "You would never let me get away with it."

"That's a fact, girl!" says Kay with a big smile. They laugh and joke together, but everyone who knows them knows that Carmen and Kay have become good friends in the time Carmen has been in the U.S.

It's still hard for Kay to believe the good times they have together in school. There was a point when she didn't think Carmen would ever leave the house!

"What are you and Jared doing tonight?" asks Kay.

"We are working with some kids at the shelter after dinner," says Carmen. "Then we may try to take in a show. How about you?"

"I'll be home by about 4:00, but I have a meeting after school."

"Oh, no," cries Carmen, "not another good cause for Miss Politics!"

They laugh. "Well, you could say that," Kay says at last. "But it's not just any old cause, and it's one you may want to help with."

"Is that right?" says Carmen. "What's this one called?"

"FSA," says Kay.

"FSA?" asks Carmen. "I don't get it."

"Friends of South America," says Kay.

And when Carmen next looks at Kay, she sees the eyes of a sister.

13. Miss Politics

"Mom, I'm home," Carmen calls out as she comes in through the kitchen door. The house seems still today. She puts her green backpack down to get a little something to eat, then heads to her room.

"There she is now," she hears Mrs. White say as she walks by the front hall.

"Are you looking for me?" asks Carmen. "I was going to my room to study for a test before Jared and I go to the shelter."

"Could you come in the living room, Carmen?" calls Mom. "There is someone here to see you."

Jared? Carmen thinks. *Robin? Mack?* She puts down her school things and goes back to the living room. At first, the woman sitting by Mom doesn't register to Carmen. It is her voice that gives her away.

"Carmen?" the woman says.

"I-I-Inez?" Carmen gets out. "Is it you?" she cries. "Is it really you?"

Carmen runs to her long-lost friend as fast as she can and puts her arms around her. They laugh and cry at the same time, just happy to be close to each other one more time.

"I was thinking I would never see you again!" cries Carmen. "I have missed you so!"

"And I was thinking the same," says Inez. "How could I find you when all I knew was that you were in California?"

"How **did** you find me?" asks Carmen, still finding it hard to believe that her friend is here.

"You will not believe it," laughs Inez, "but I looked at the news one night and saw the news woman talking to a girl. Your face had changed a little, but I knew your voice, I knew your eyes, and I cried when I heard your name."

"Oh, Inez, I'm so happy you are here," says Carmen, her eyes growing wet. "When did you get to the U.S.? And how?"

"That part of the story is good," says Inez. "You see, I was thinking my boyfriend Luis had died in South America, but **I was wrong**. When he got away, he just made his way from camp to camp and found me!"

"What about your family?" Carmen wants to know.

"There is no word on them so far, Carmen, but remember what I told you in camp? Never, **never** give up hope. I have not," Inez smiles. "It was not safe for us to stay in South America. We got married, Luis and I, and an American friend of his helped us get to the U.S."

Carmen sits back and looks at her friend, and can't believe how happy she is to see her **and** to hear the words of a South American. Then, seeing that Mom has not understood anything that they have been talking about, Carmen tells Mrs. White about Inez.

Turning back to Inez, Carmen asks the hard question that is on her mind: "Do you really think there is any way that our families — my family — may still be alive, Inez?"

"Yes, I do," Inez says with a smile. "We are finding that some people did **not** die on that night in the fields. But it will take a lot of hard work and some time to get all the answers we need."

"Well," says Carmen, looking at Mrs. White with a big smile, "I think we know just the girl for the job. In fact, she has started working on it even now with a group called Friends of South America."

"What is her name?" Inez asks.

"At school," laughs Carmen, "we know her as 'Miss Politics.' Around the house, we just call her Kay."

14. Back to Work

"Nothing but **nothing** puts new life into Kay White like a new cause!" laughs Jared as the FSA group works into the night in the Whites' kitchen.

"We are making some headway too," Kay tells them. "We don't know about the Cruz family so far, but we are finding a lot of people in the meantime."

While Inez and her husband make calls to raise money for the work ahead, the others put letters together to go out the next day. Carmen looks at Jared, who has been one of the biggest FSA workers from the start. He, Carmen, and Kay have taken a break from Friends 4 Life, now that the playground is in, to put some time into Friends of South America. As she looks at him, Jared sees her and smiles.

"What are you smiling at?" says Mom, walking over to Carmen. "Or should I say **who**?"

"I'm just thinking about how happy I am now," Carmen says. "I used to think I had no life anymore. My mom used to tell me that I would go far and do big things, but I told her she was wrong."

"And now?" asks Mrs. White.

"Now I know that I'm going to do the biggest thing of all," Carmen tells her. "I want to find my family."

"I know," says Mom. "We are all happy for you, and we all want to help."

"I want you to know something," Carmen goes on, her eyes on this woman she cares for so much. "Even if, somehow, I don't find them, I have found a new life here. I am happy again. I can smile again. And I know that my mom was right. I **will** go far, and I **will** do big things."

Now it is Mom's turn to cry. "I knew that all along," she says, taking Carmen's hand, "from the day I found you in the camp. It was **you** who needed to find it out for yourself, Carmen."

"All right, you two," says Kay, walking over with a pack of letters in each hand, "are we going to talk and cry all day, or are we going to get back to work here?"

"You win, Miss Politics," laugh Mom and Carmen.

"Just point me in the right direction," Carmen says. "After all, there is a planet to save!"